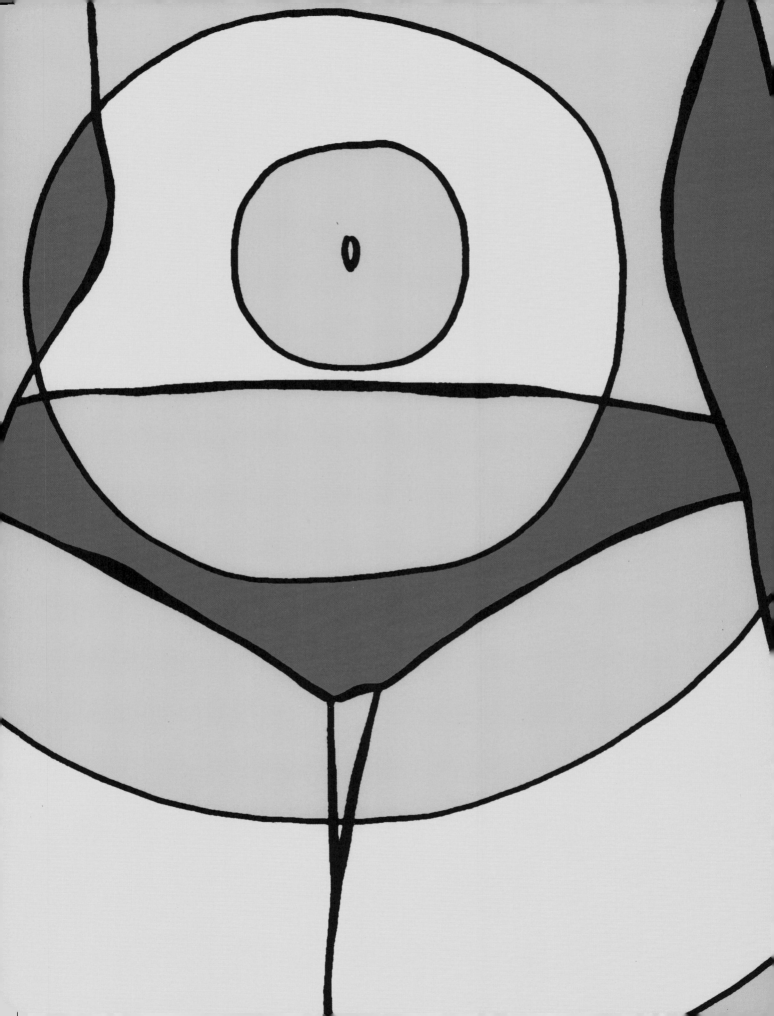

Fantagraphics Books Inc. ♦ 7563 Lake City Way NE ♦ Seattle, Washington, 98115 ♦ Editor and Associate
Publisher: Eric Reynolds ♦ Book Design: Keeli McCarthy ♦ Production: Paul Baresh ♦ Publisher: Gary Groth
My Pretty Vampire is copyright © 2017 Katie Skelly. This edition is copyright © 2017 Fantagraphics Books Inc.
Permission to reproduce content must be obtained from the author or publisher. ♦ ISBN 978-1-68396-020-1
Library of Congress Control Number: 2016961136 ♦ First printing: August 2017 ♦ Printed in Hong Kong

MY PRETTY VAMPIRE

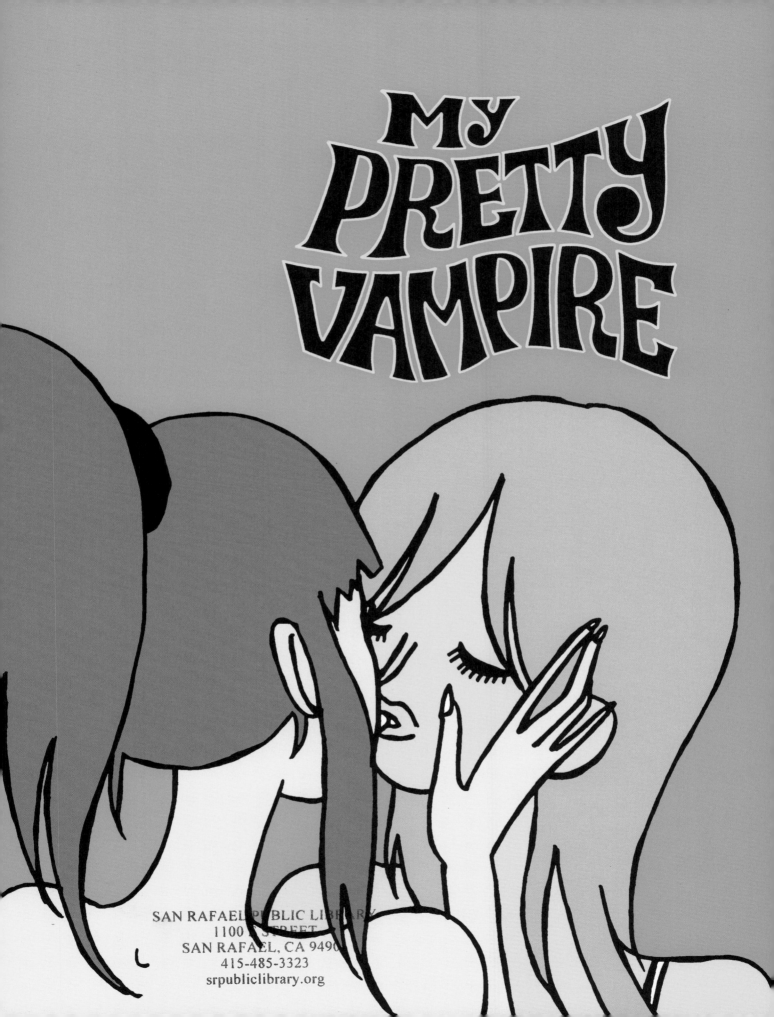

CHAPTER ONE

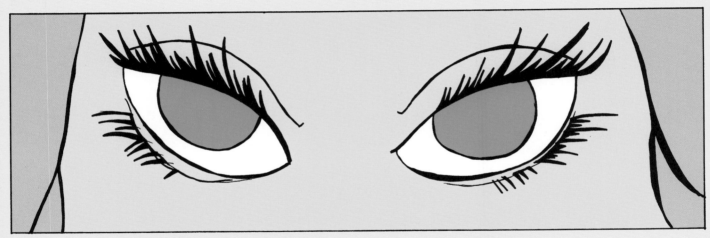

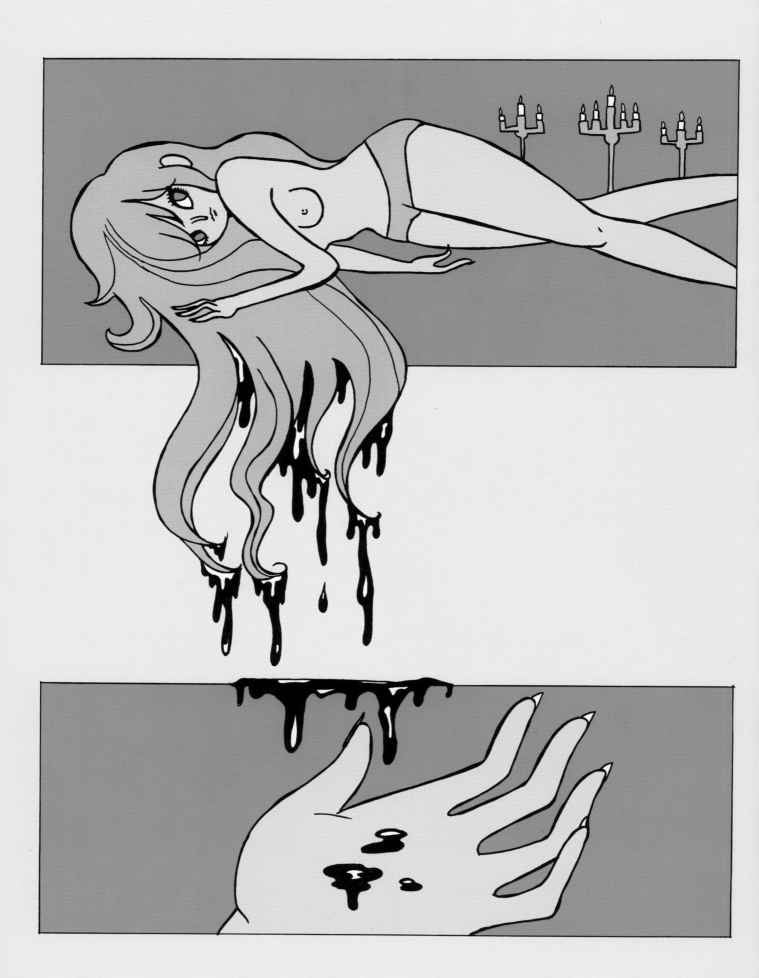

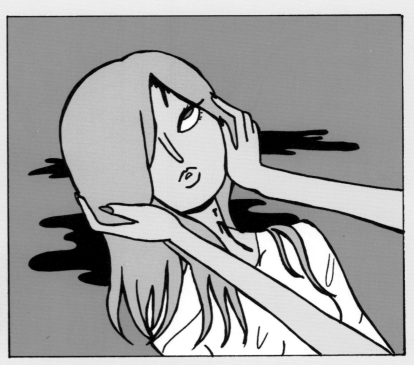

IT'S TIME TO WAKE UP, ANYWAY.
GOOD MORNING.
CLOVER...
PLEASE TRY TO STUDY TODAY.

SURE...
NNN...
WAIT...

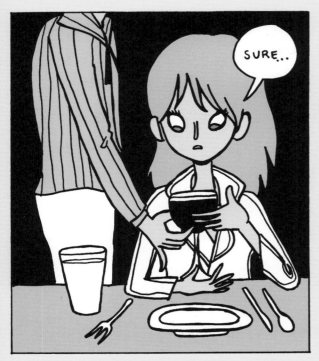

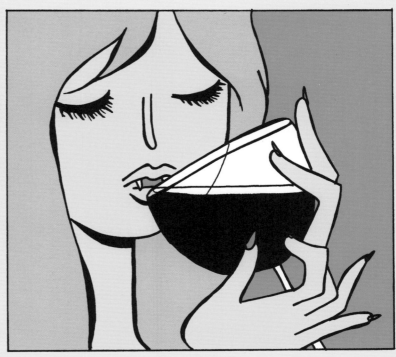

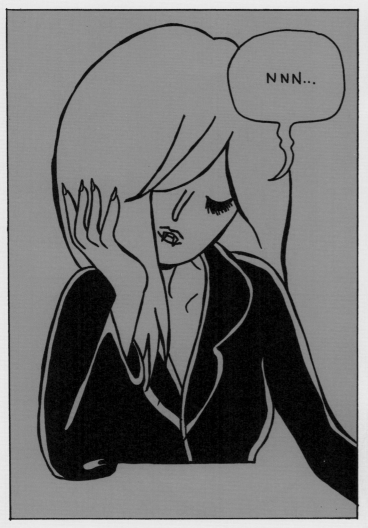

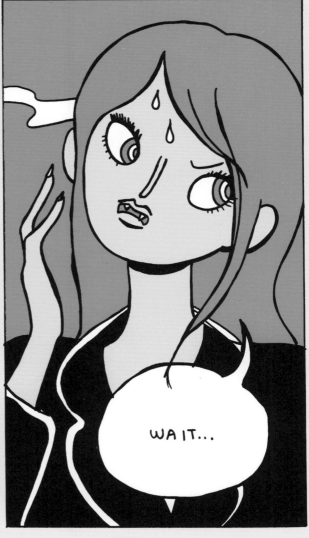

WHAT IS THIS?!
OX BLOOD. YOU KNOW THAT.
IT'S NOT THAT BAD...
COUGH
I CAN'T LIVE LIKE THIS!
I'M SICK, MARCEL!
YOU HAVE TO!
NO ONE ELSE WILL TAKE CARE OF YOU...
IT'S JUST US.

FUCK OFF!
I HATE HIM!
HE'S NOT MY BROTHER, HE'S A PERVERT!
AND I'M STARVING!

IT'S BEEN ALMOST FOUR YEARS...
SOB
... SINCE I WAS BIT.
FOUR YEARS AND I CAN'T EVEN SEE WHERE I WAS BITTEN!
SIGH

STUPID FUCKING "UNIFORM"...
OH!
ELSA!
SHH..!
I HAFF
SOMETHING...
WOW! THANK YOU...
BE VELL, CLOVER.
CLOSE

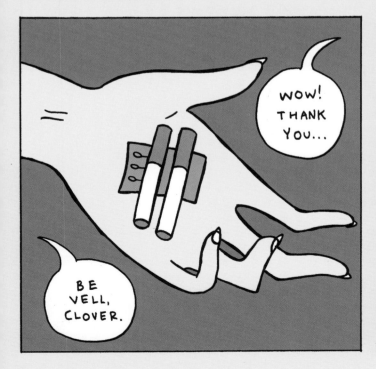

CLICK
DIARY
my escape
TO BE CONT'D
KS

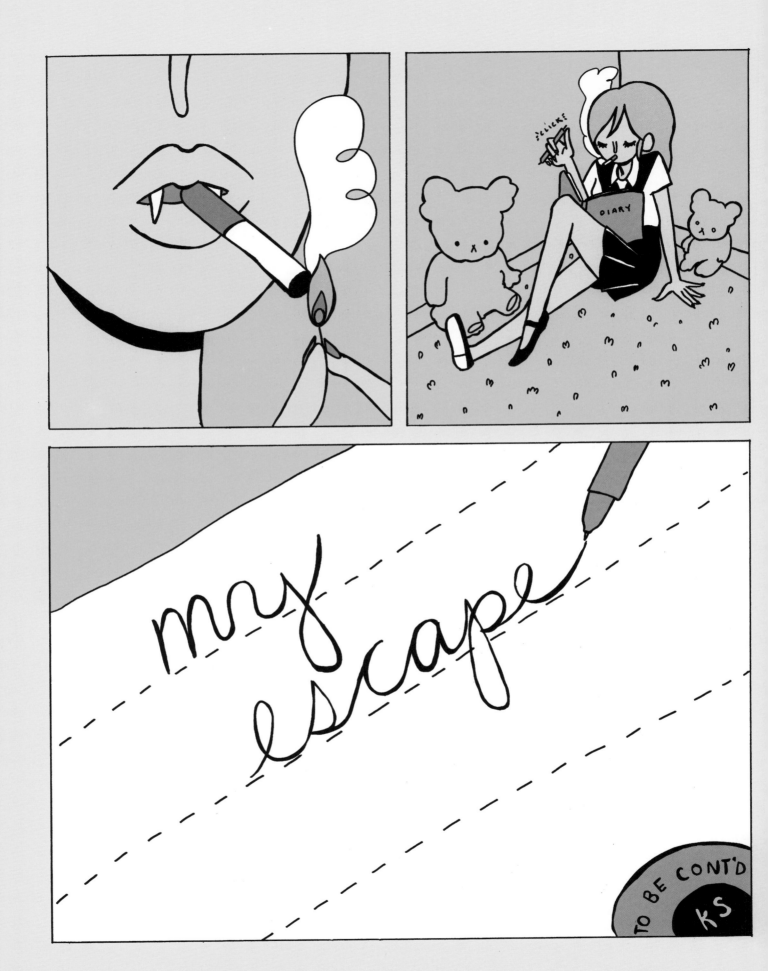

CHAPTER TWO

CLICK
CLACK
CLICK
CLACK
CLICK

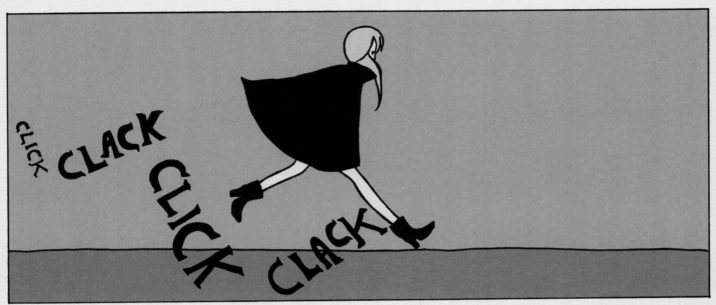

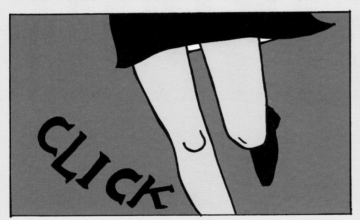

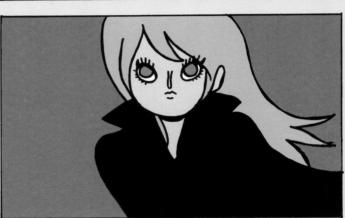

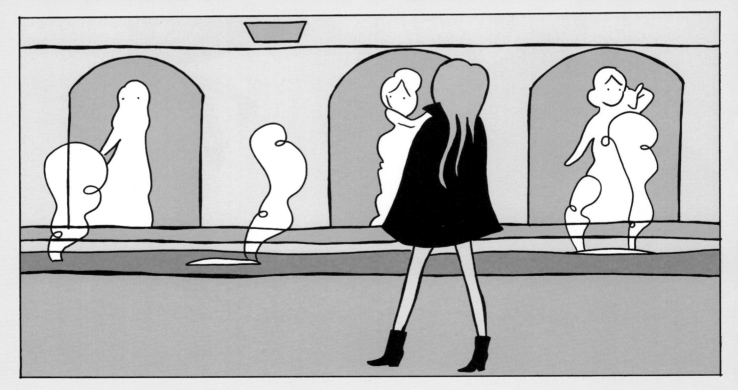

ALMOST... THERE...

GASP!

CLOVER! STOP! WHAT ARE YOU DOING?
YOU'LL GET HURT! YOU'LL BE HUNTED!
LET GO!
PLEASE...
KISS
NO--!!

UNF!!
PANT
I'M SO WEAK...
HUNGRY...

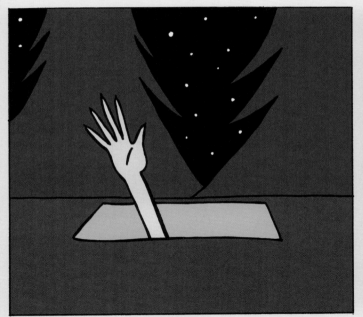

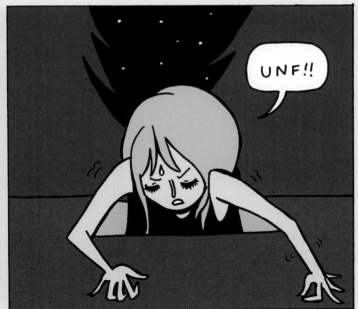

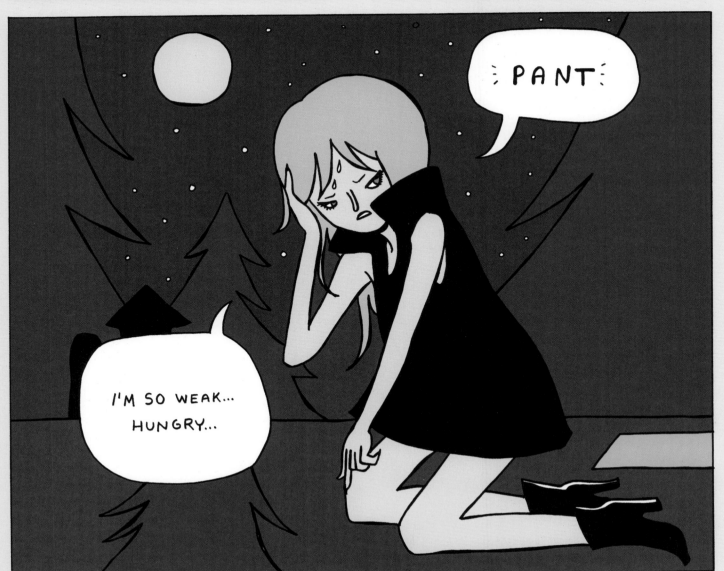

BANG!

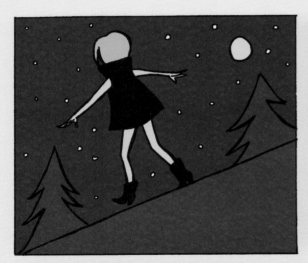

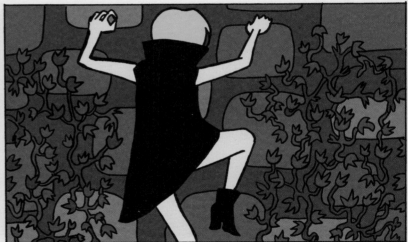

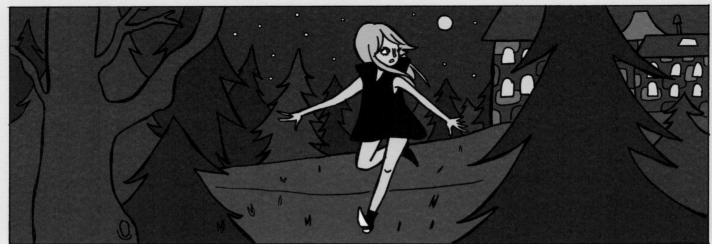

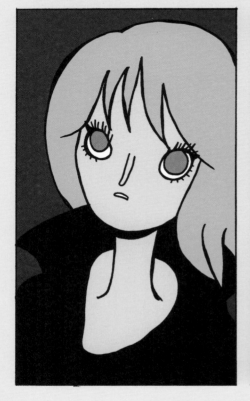

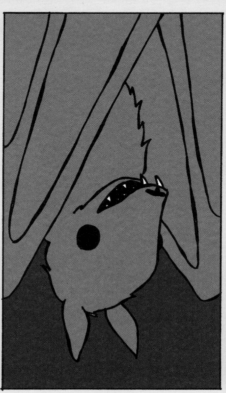

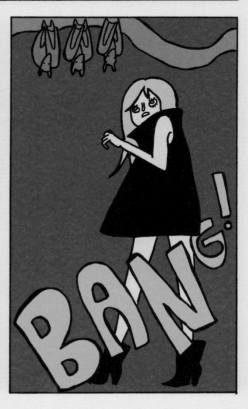

WHERE ARE YOU?!
BANG!
CLOVER!
BANG!
BANG!
SHH...
CLICK
CLACK

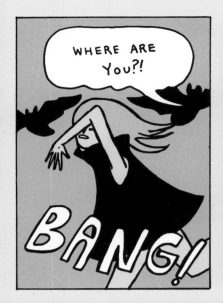

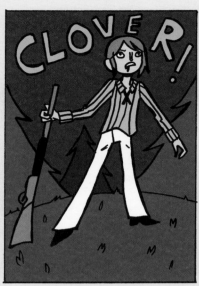

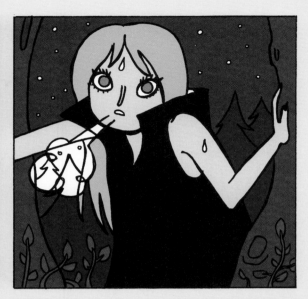

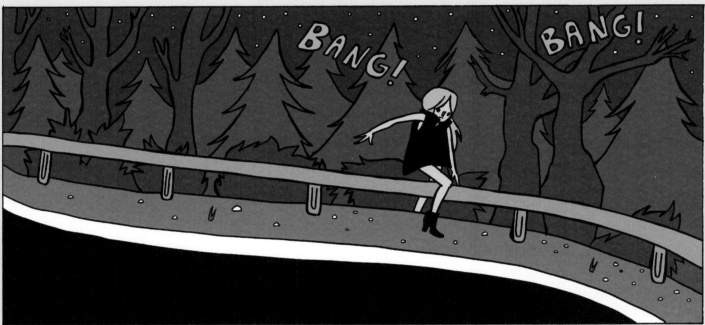

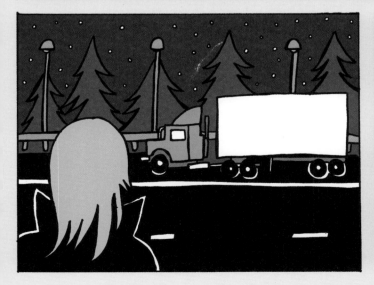

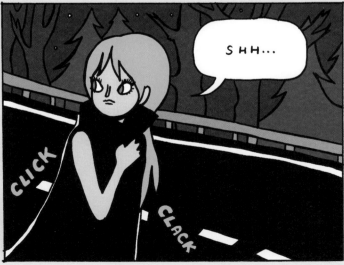

KNOCK KNOCK
THE FUCK...
WHAT DO YOU WANT?
MAY I COME IN?
THANK YOU.

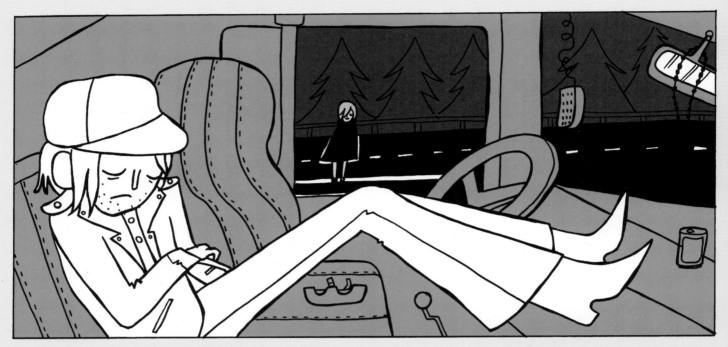

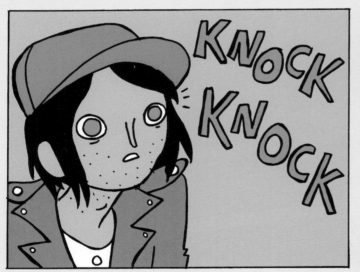

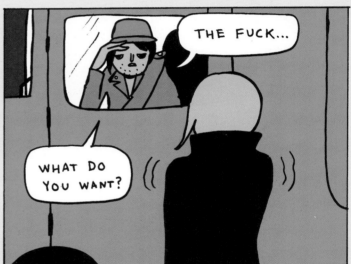

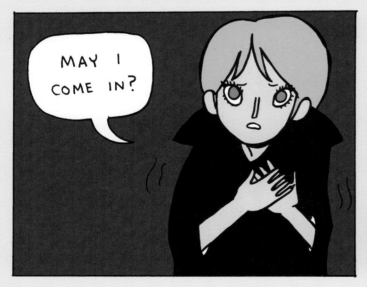

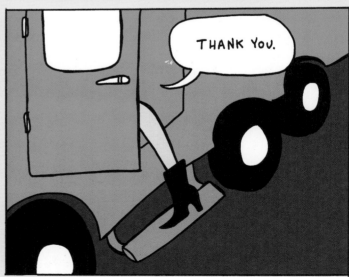

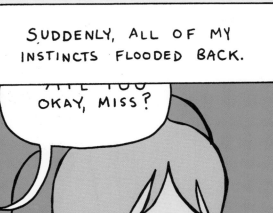

SUDDENLY, ALL OF MY INSTINCTS FLOODED BACK.

ARE YOU OKAY, MISS?

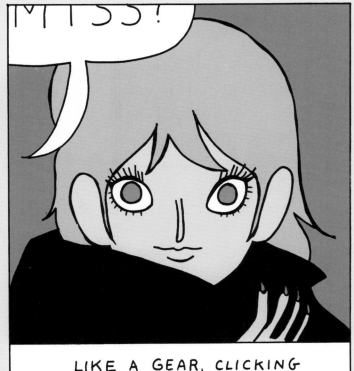

MISS?

LIKE A GEAR, CLICKING BACK INTO PLACE.

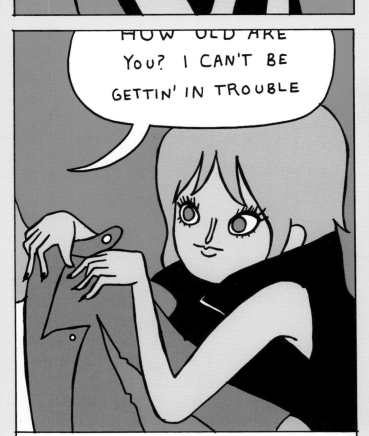

HOW OLD ARE YOU? I CAN'T BE GETTIN' IN TROUBLE

CLICK...

CLICK.

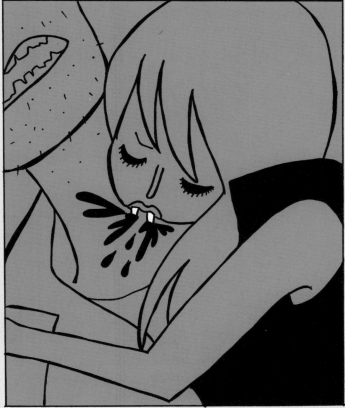
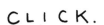

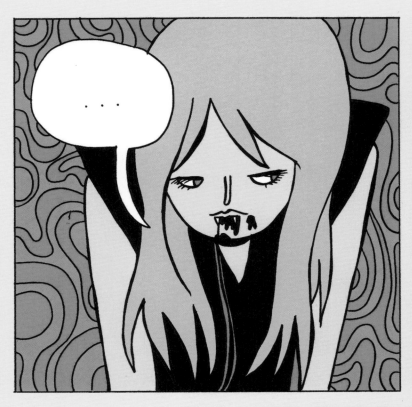

. . .

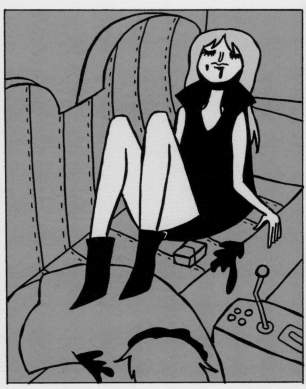

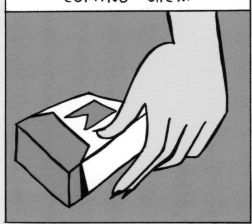

MY STRENGTH IS COMING BACK.

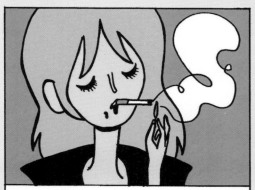

MY MIND FEELS SHARPER, TOO.

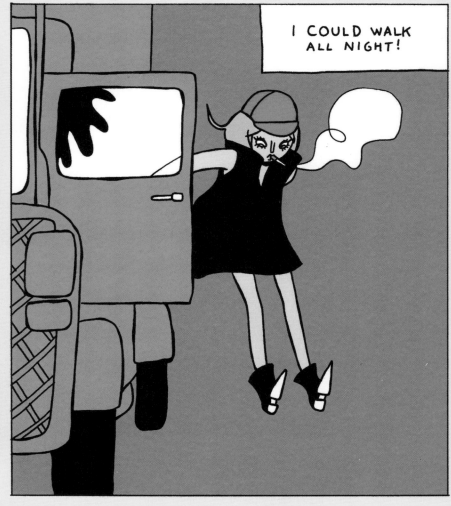

I COULD WALK ALL NIGHT!

I NEED A PLAN.
MARCEL WILL LOOK FOR ME.
I HAVE NO MONEY...
I SHOULD'VE CHECKED THE TRUCKER...
DAMN.
30 MI.
I HAVE TO BE SMARTER OUT HERE!

MR. MARCEL?
DO YOU NEED ANYFING ELSE TONIGHT?
...
GET OUT!
GET OUT!
SEE YOU MONDAY.

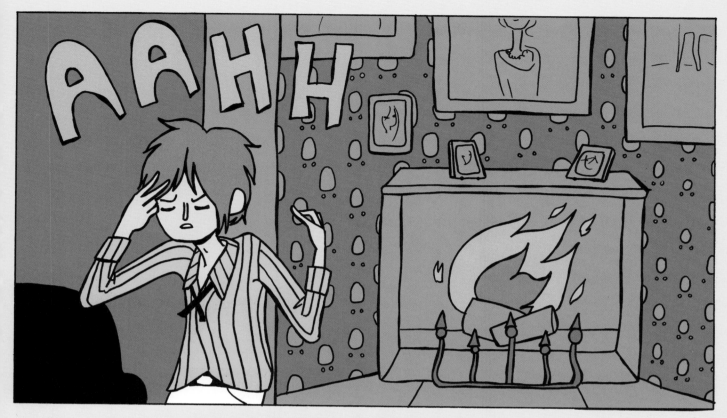

I CAN'T BELIEVE THAT THIS HAPPENED...

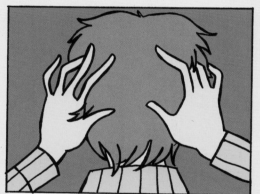

I WAS ABLE TO KEEP HER FOUR YEARS...

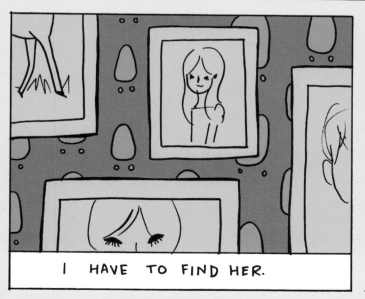

I HAVE TO FIND HER.

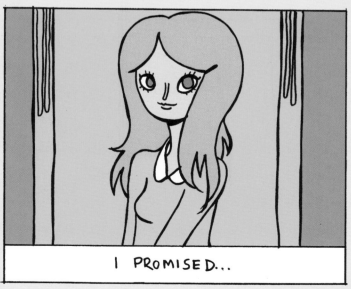

I PROMISED...

I PROMISED...
CREEP
MAY I COME IN?
TO BE CONT'D
KS

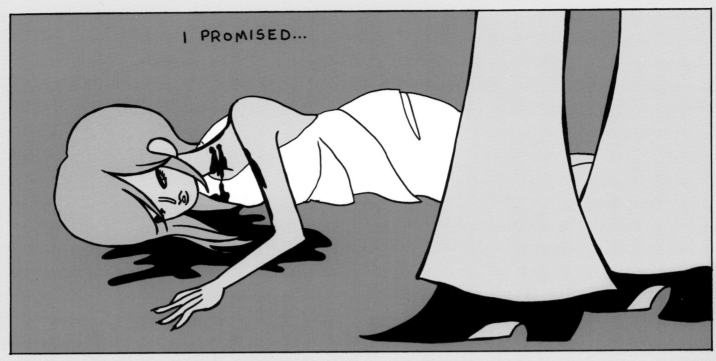

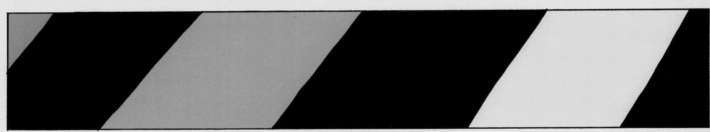

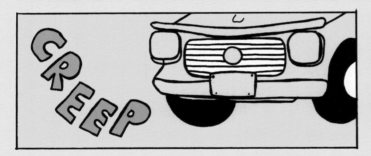

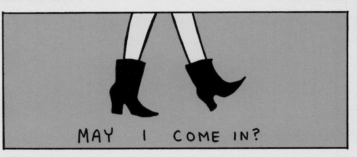

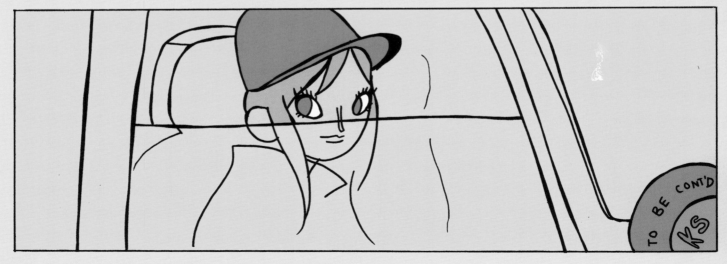

CHAPTER THREE

HELLO?
—HELLO?!
I -- DON'T—
KNOW WHAT TO DO!
SHE'S GONE...

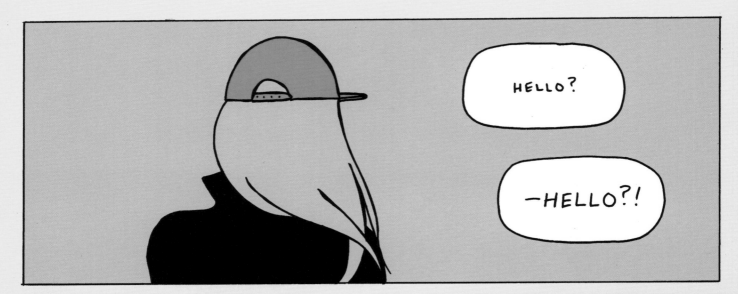

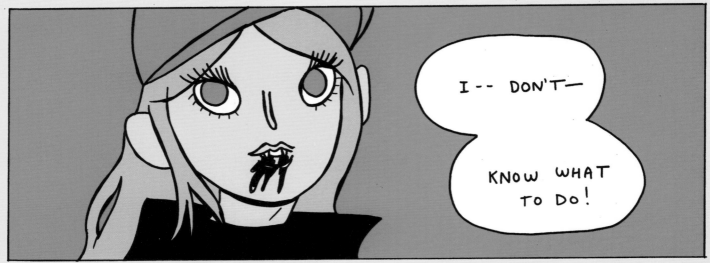

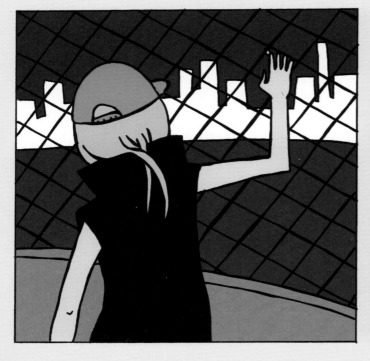

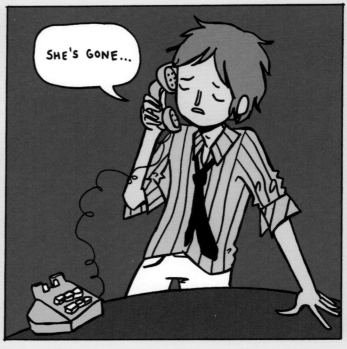

HOW LONG?
4 HOURS.
HOW WOULD YOU LIKE TO PROCEED?
BILL ME FOR YOUR OTHER CASES.
IT'S URGENT.
ANNE WILL INVOICE YOU.
CLANG

KEE
OU
ICHABOD
HEY!

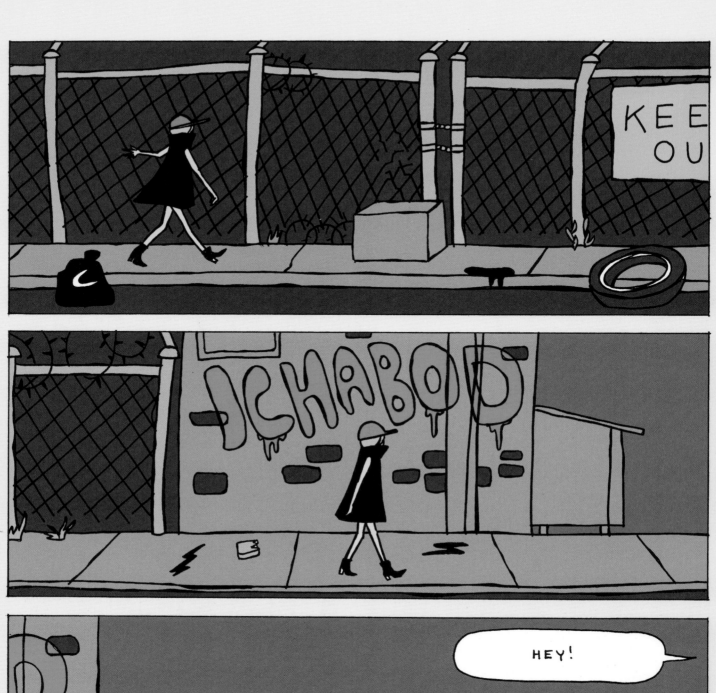

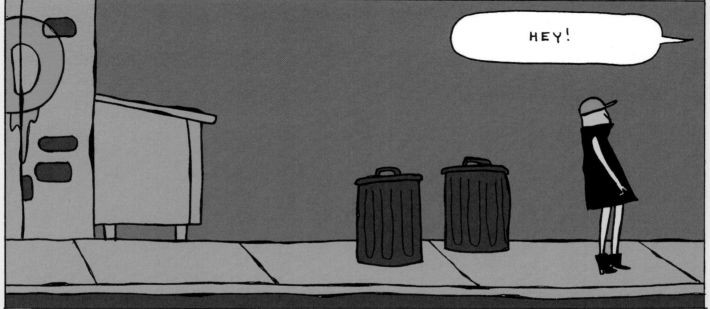

HURRY UP!
JESUS...
STUPID DOG...
RRR

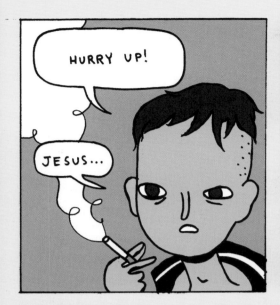

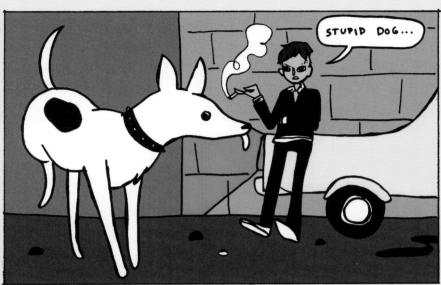

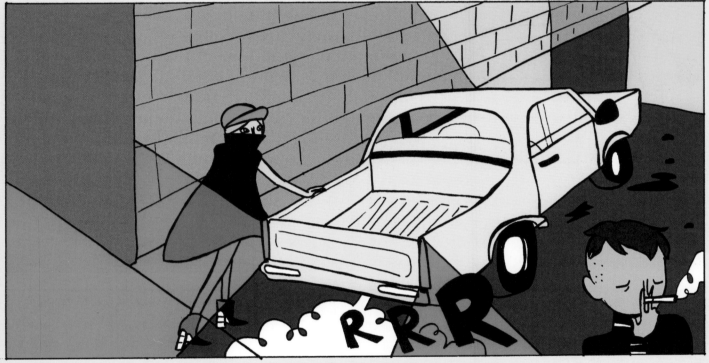

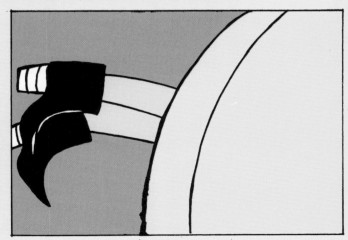

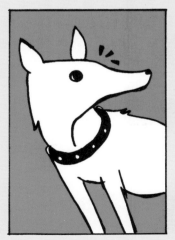

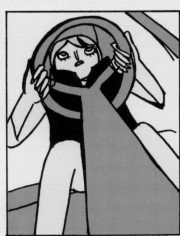

YAP! YAP!
THE FUCK?
WHOA! WHOA!!

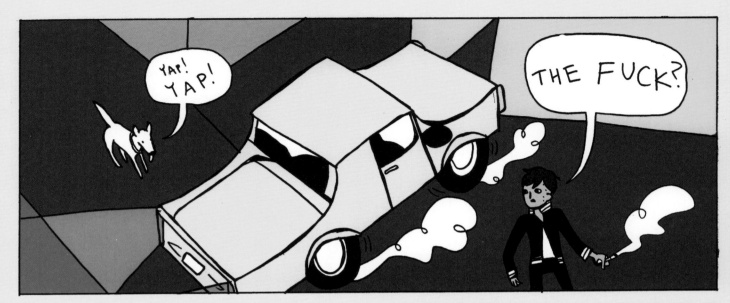

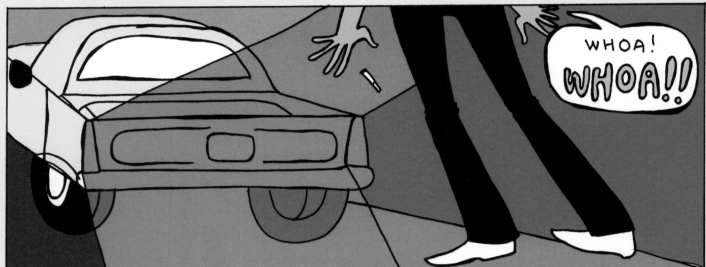

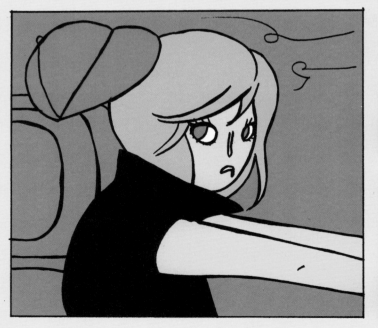

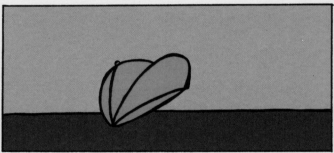

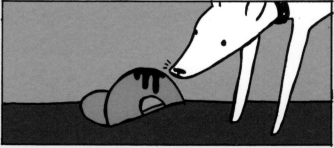

SCREEE
FUCK.

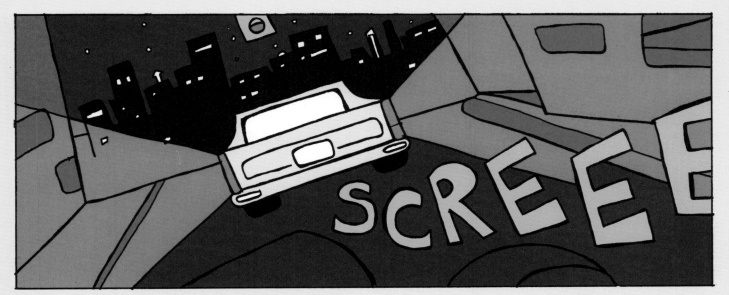

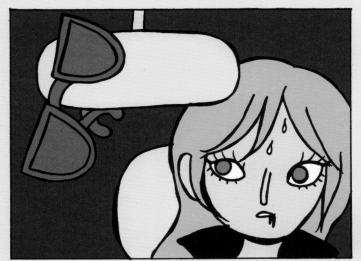

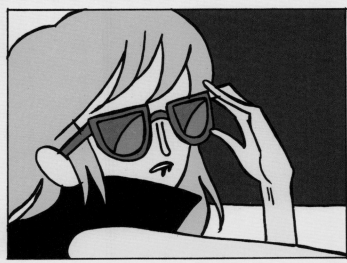

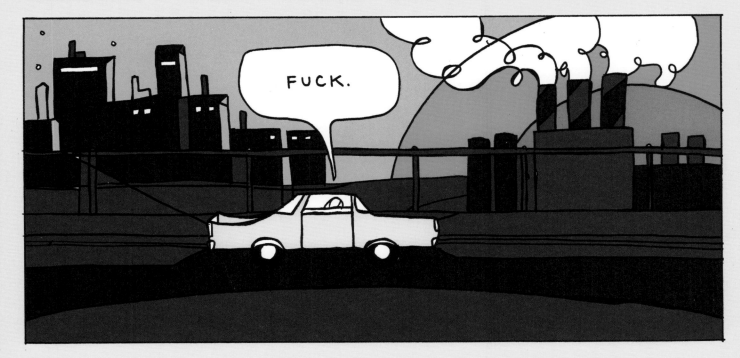

GET THE WINDSHIELD.
HEY, OFFICER.
JOHN! MISSIN' THE FORCE AGAIN, HUH?
I GOT ANOTHER RUNAWAY RICH KID.
WHAT'S GOING ON HERE?
TRUCK DRIVER. NO SIGN OF ROBBERY.
TOTALLY BLED OUT. WEIRD SHIT.
WHY THIS GUY? NO RECORD, NO MONEY. STRANGE.

SO THAT'S ONE BODY DOWN.
OR TWO.
FUCK!

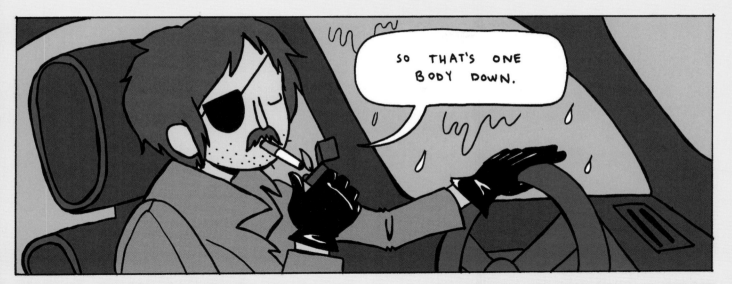

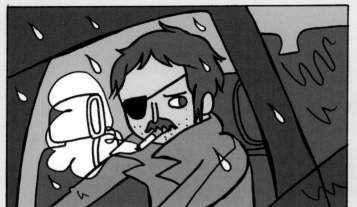

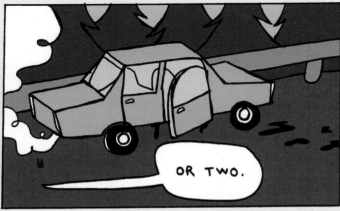

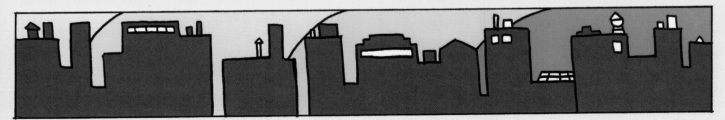

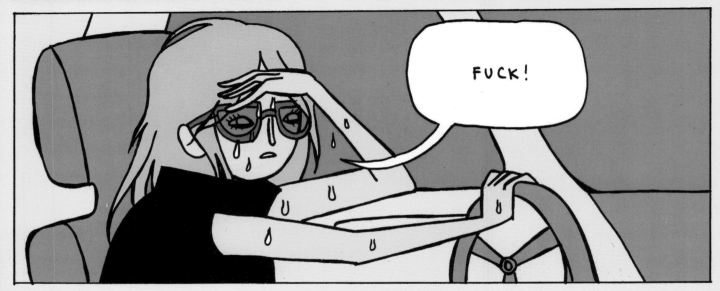

RING!
YES?!
COUPLE BODIES DOWN. YOUR SISTER'S ON THE WARPATH.
JESUS...
I'LL SEE IF I CAN FIND WHERE SHE'S HOLED UP, ASSUMING SHE'S NOT FRIED...

GASP!

UNF...
HAVE TO BE MORE CAREFUL OF THE SUN...
I'LL JUST HIDE HERE AWHILE...
IT'S SO... QUIET...
!
NO!

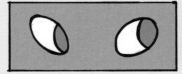

NO NO NO!

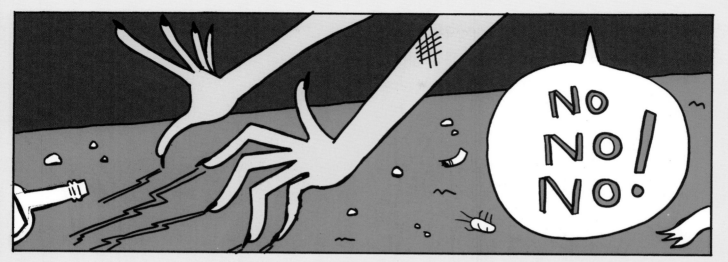

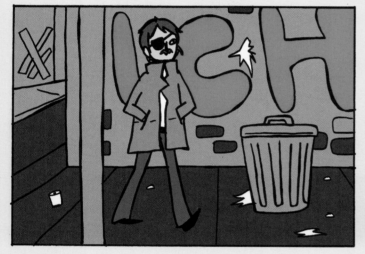

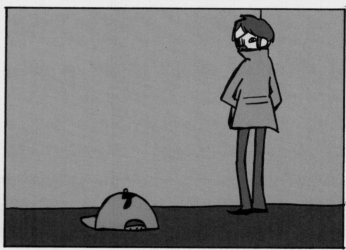

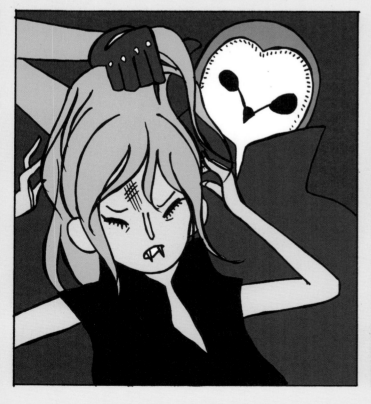

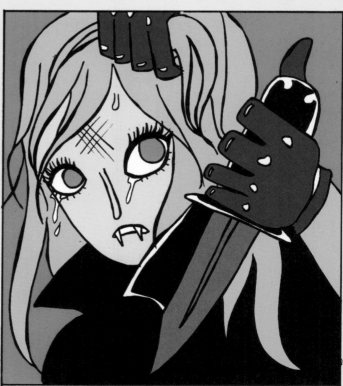

DOES... ANYONE ELSE KNOW SHE'S LOOSE?
THE ORDER? DON'T BELIEVE SO. THEN AGAIN, WE WOULD NEVER KNOW.
PHO
BUT I DOUBT IT. JUST HANG TIGHT.
WE'LL FIND HER.
to be cont'd

CHAPTER FOUR

KISS IT.
GO ON.

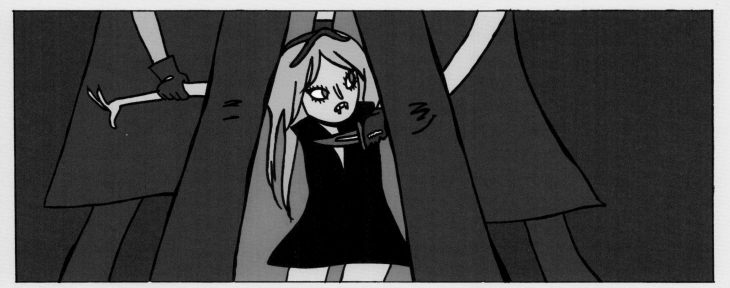

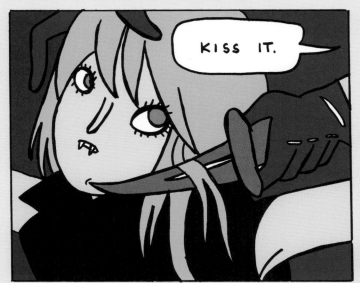

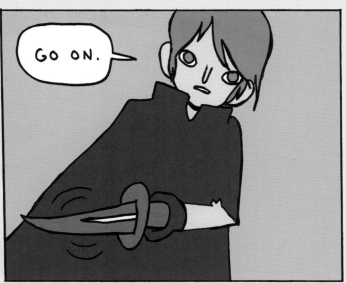

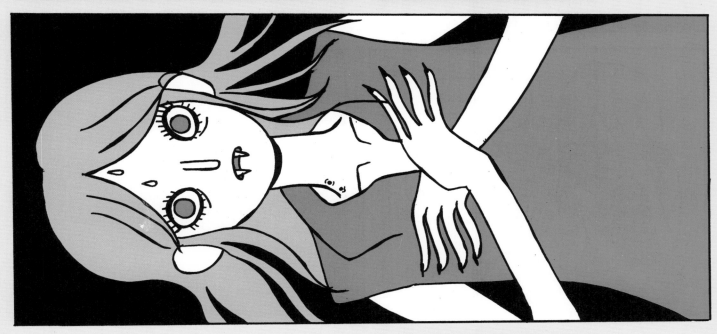

A DREAM!
MY BLOOD BETRAYS ME...
EVEN MY DREAMS BETRAY ME!
BLUH HUH HUH...
I'M HUNGRY AGAIN, TOO...
RUMBLE
SUN'S DOWN AGAIN... I MUST HAVE SLEPT FOR A LONG TIME.

NOWHERE
HA HA HA HA

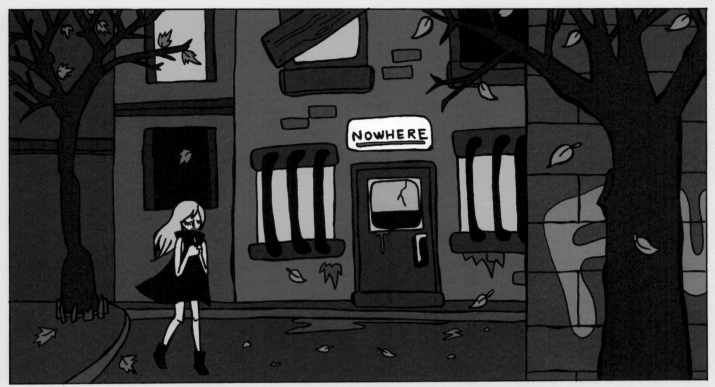

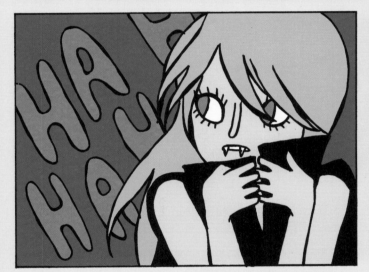

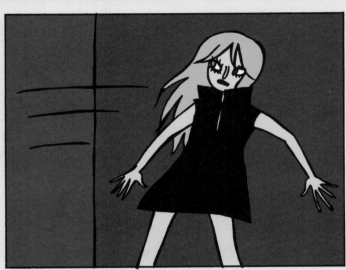

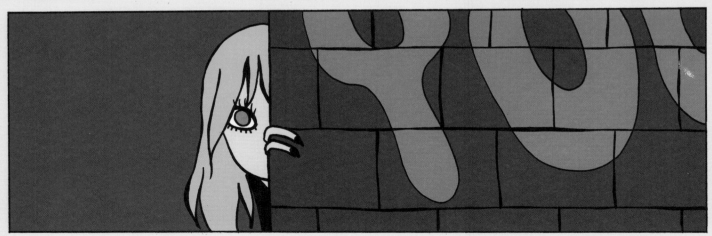

NOWHERE
HA HA
SLOW DOWN...
HEY!
NOT OUT HERE!
JESUS...
WHAT THE FUCK?!
THE CUSTOMER IS ALWAYS RIGHT, HUH?

I'M SORRY, BABY... THEY'RE NOT MY RULES...
AW, I UNDERSTAND...
...
RUMBLE
ALMOST THERE...
WHERE'D HE GO?!

FUCK.

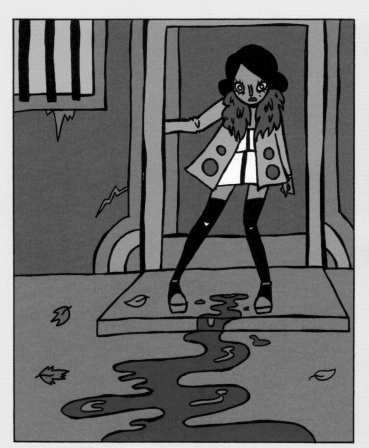

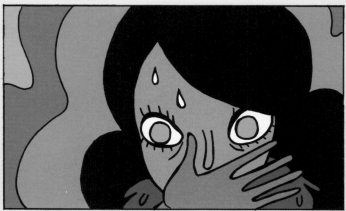

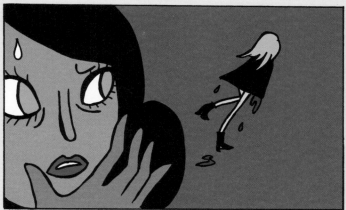

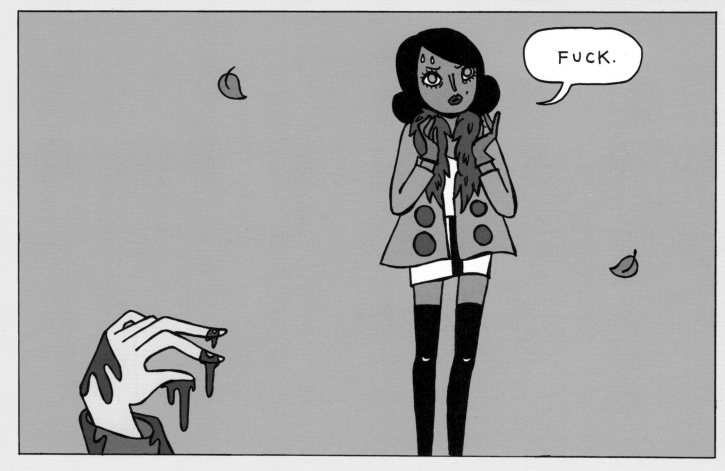

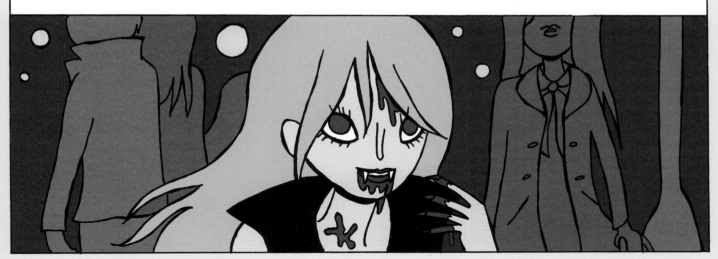

MY ENERGY IS BACK!

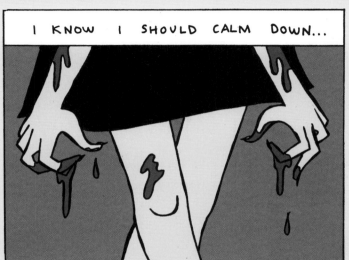

I KNOW I SHOULD CALM DOWN...

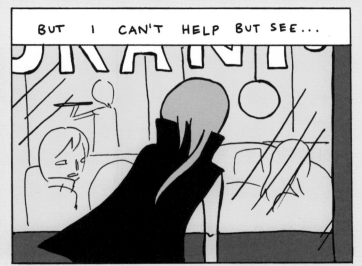

BUT I CAN'T HELP BUT SEE...

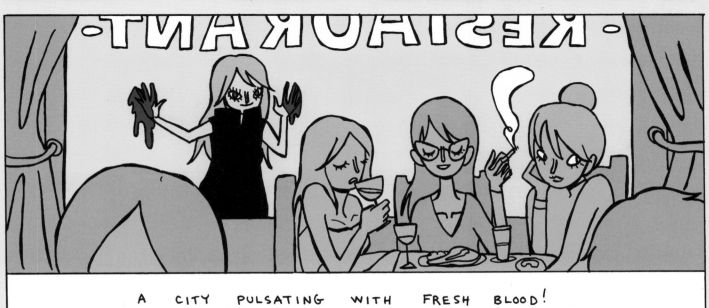

A CITY PULSATING WITH FRESH BLOOD!

SQUEAK
NOWHERE
N
21
POST

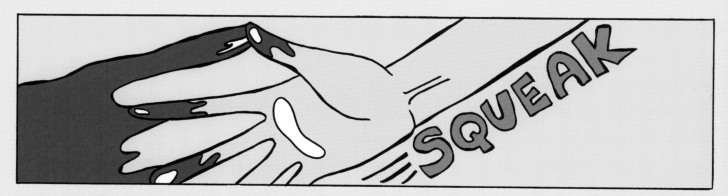

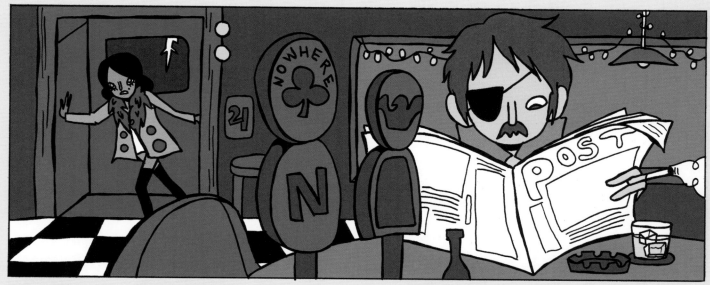

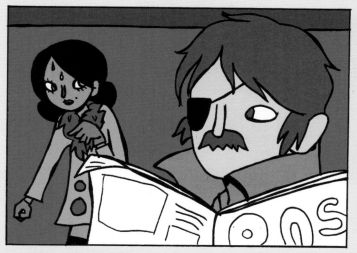

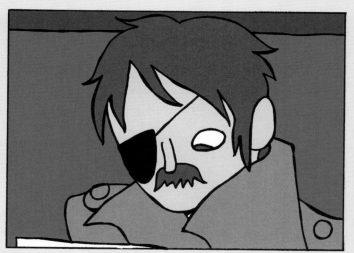

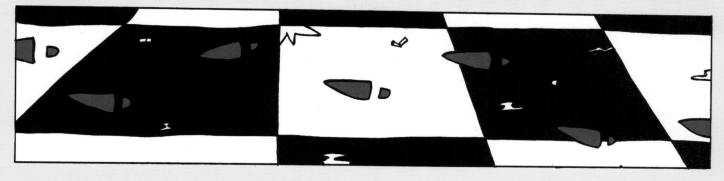

SEE SOMETHING YOU LIKE?
SHE'S GREAT.
EMPLOYEES ONLY
NOT TONIGHT, THANKS.

BINGO.
TO BE CONT'D

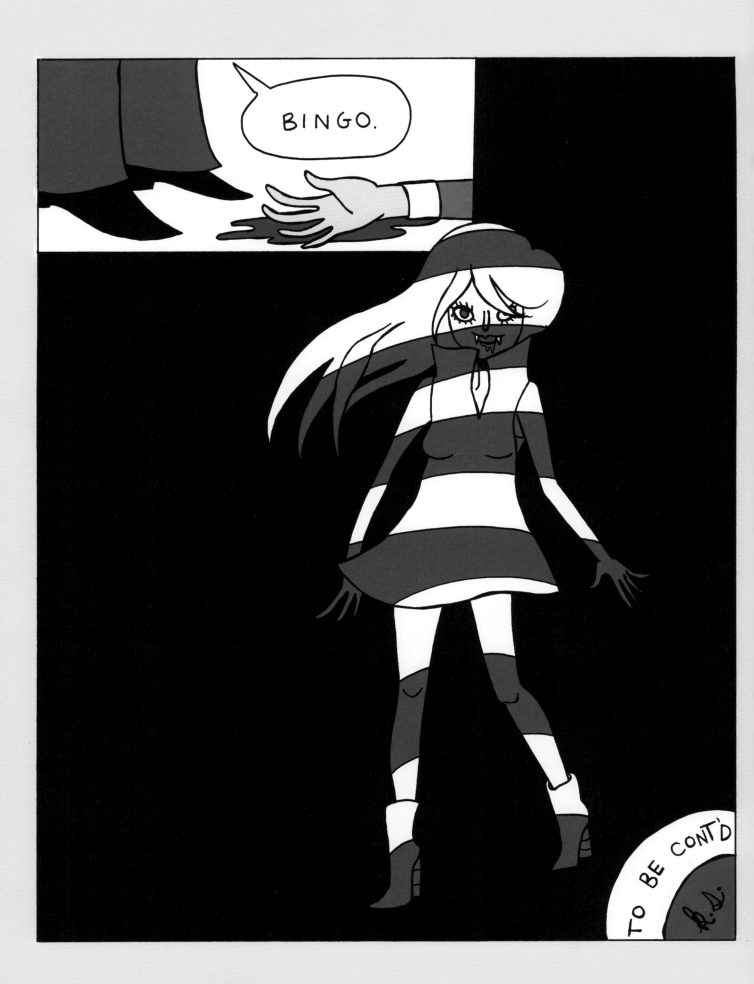

CHAPTER FIVE

HAHAHAHAHA
MEW?
GASP!
HISSSSSS!!

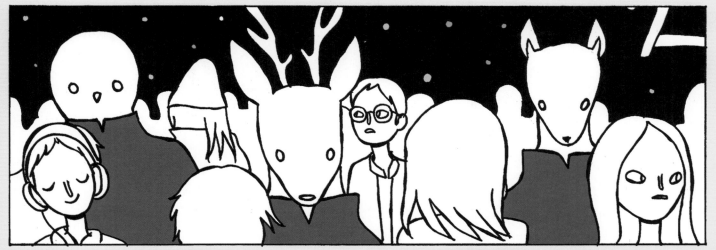

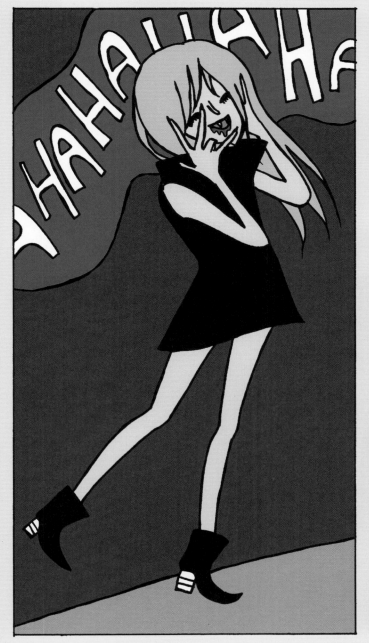

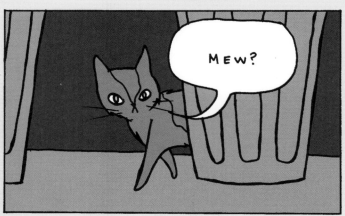

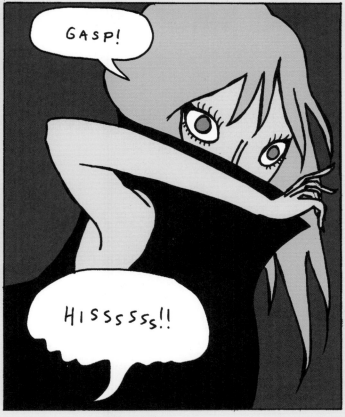

HISSSSs!!!
WIPE
Iron + Oak

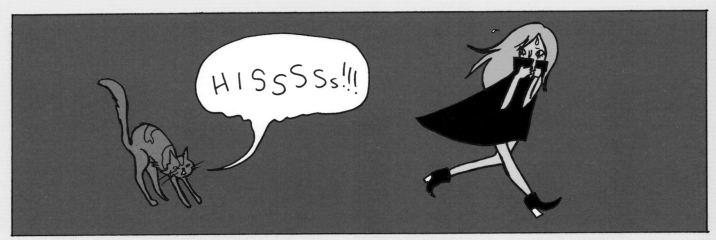

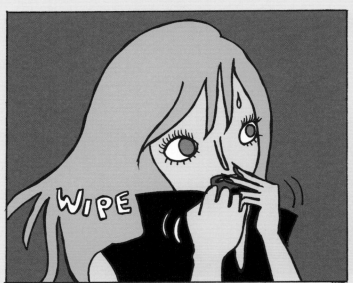

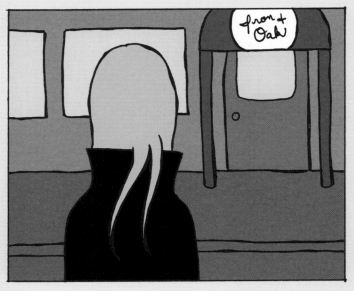

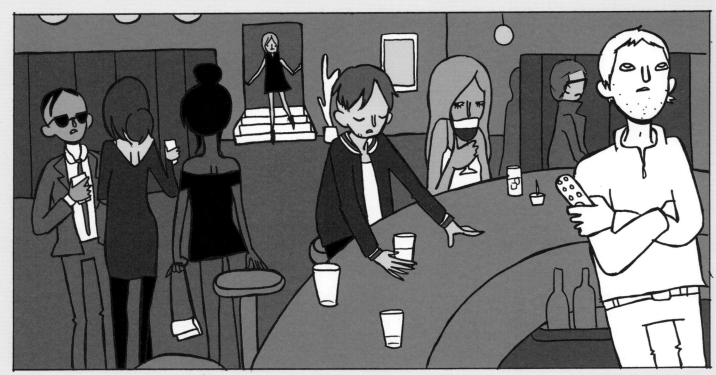

NOW BACK TO THOSE GRISLY DOWNTOWN MURDERS-
7
TURN THAT UP!
AN UNIDENTIFIED MAN WAS FOUND DEAD WITH MULTIPLE STAB WOUNDS AT ABOUT 10 PM TONIGHT.
POLIC
VOL
POLICE ARE LOOKING INTO CONNECTIONS TO THE INTERSTATE MURDERS EARLIER THIS WEEK—
—PLEASE CALL THE 17TH PRECINCT WITH ANY INFORMATION—

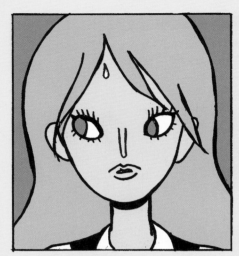
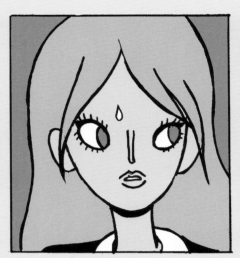
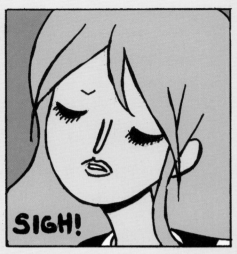

SIGH!

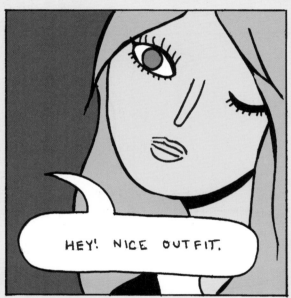

HEY! NICE OUTFIT.

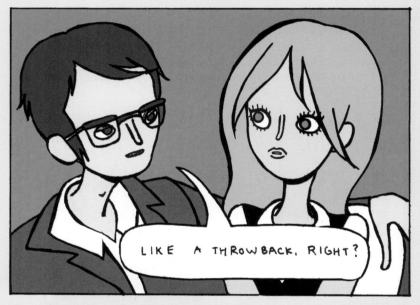

LIKE A THROWBACK, RIGHT?

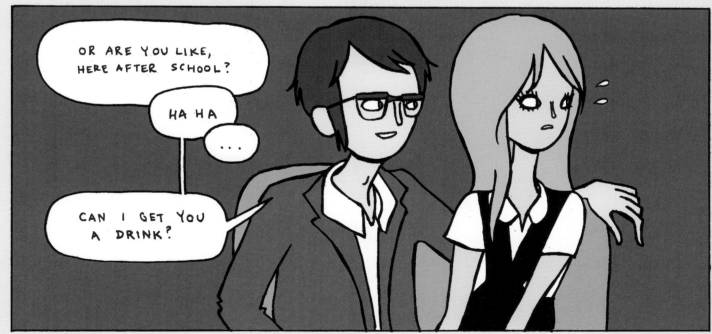

OR ARE YOU LIKE, HERE AFTER SCHOOL?

HA HA

...

CAN I GET YOU A DRINK?

5 YEARS AGO...

"MOST PEOPLE THAT COME TO US WANT MONEY, POWER...

...ETERNAL LIFE, FOR THEMSELVES.

NOT YOU.

YOU DID IT OUT OF LOVE.

THE ONE YOU LOVE WILL NEVER DIE.

(HOW SELFISH.)

KEEP HER SAFE...

HISSSSSS...

OR WE WILL."

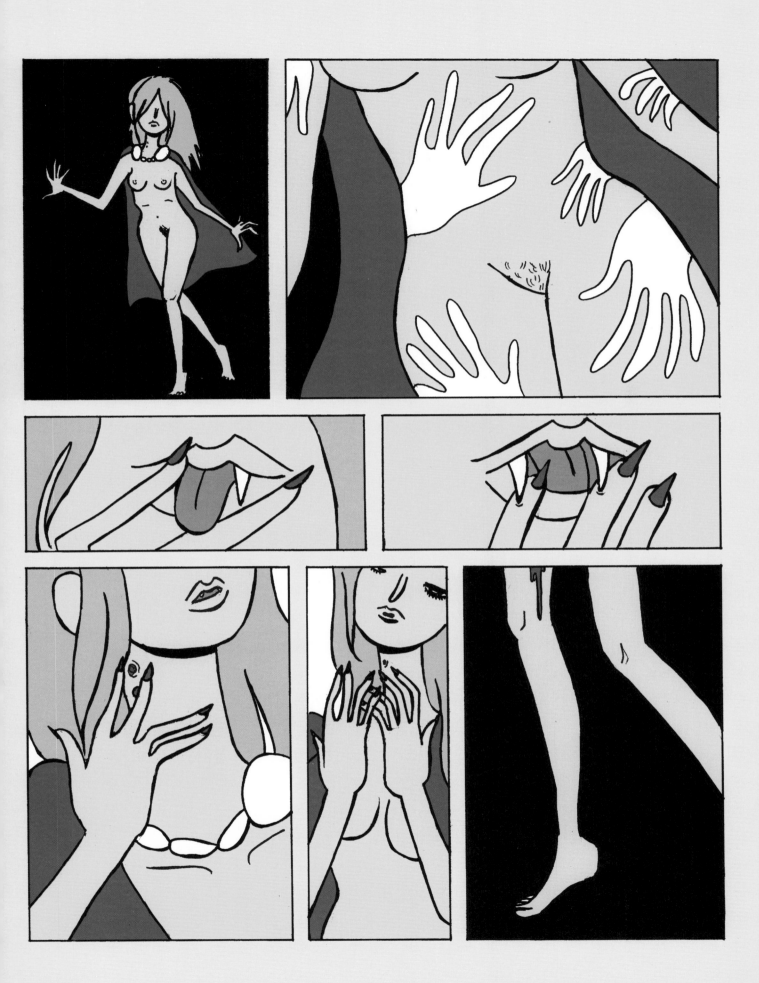

HISSSSSSSss

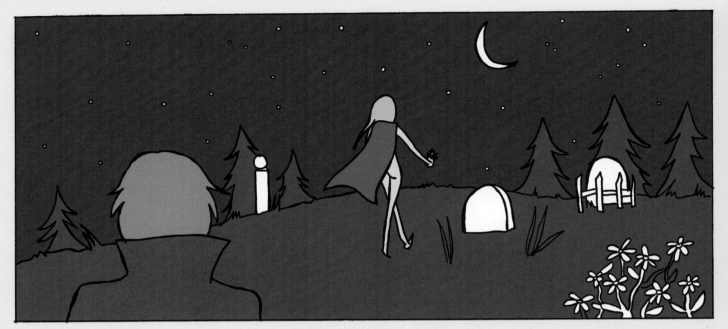

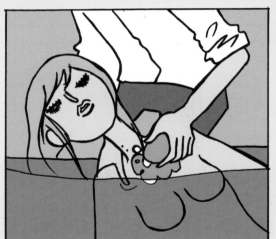

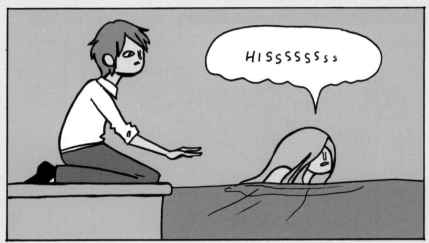

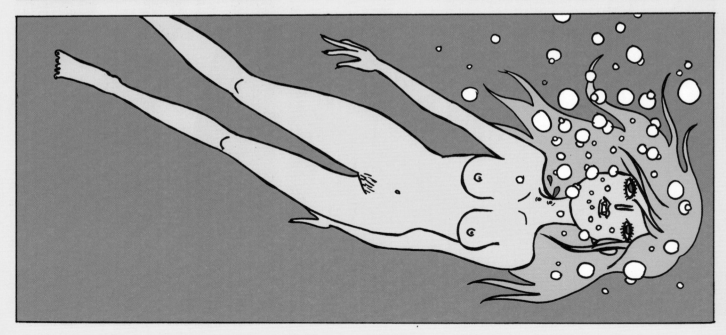

...DO YOU SPEAK ENGLISH?
WHAT ARE YOU DOING LATER?
I'M HAVING A LITTLE PARTY AT MY PLACE...
DO YOU WANT TO COME?
...
NOD NOD

7 8 9
4 5 6
1 2 3
DING!
woo!
WHO'S THERE?
HOPE YOU BROUGHT MORE DRUGS... SHEILA'S A VACUUM...
SORRY NOT SORRY!

...MAY I COME IN?
YES, OF COURSE...
HI! YOUR HAIR IS GORGEOUS...
WHAT'S YOUR NAME?
CLOVER...
READY TO PARTY? COME ON!
HERE WE GO...

HOW DO YOU KNOW DAVID?
POP!
I DON'T, REALLY...
WELL, TO NEW FRIENDS, THEN...
DRINK UP!
HEE HEE...
FOUND MY SECRET STASH!

SNIFF
HERE, BABE.
TRY IT.
THERE YOU GO...
I WANNA TRY YOUR DRESS ON...
WHAT?
OH...

HA HA!
I LOOK GREAT!
DON'T YOU THINK?
RUMBLE...

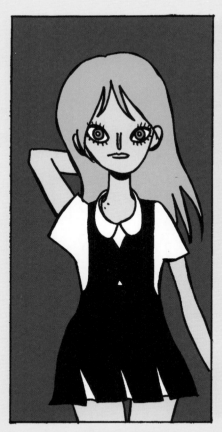

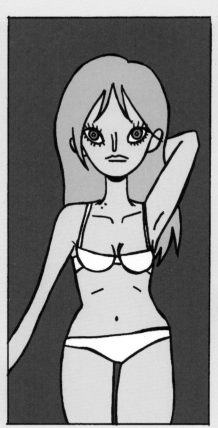

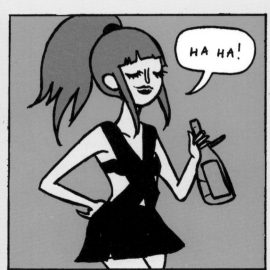

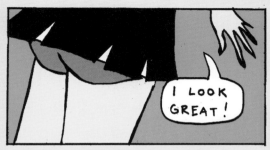

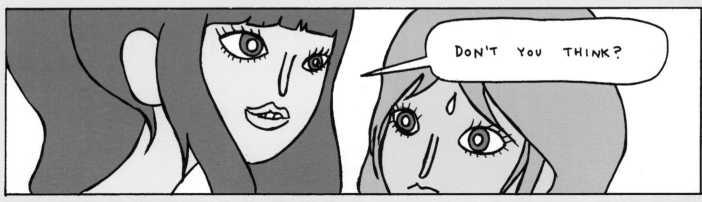

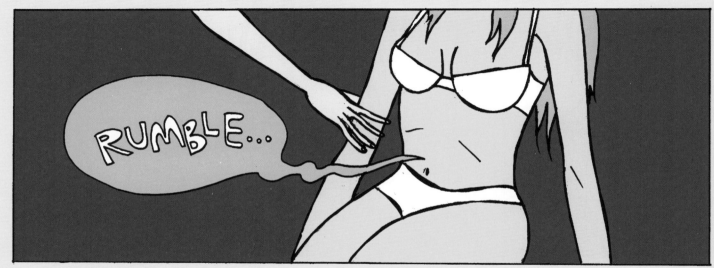

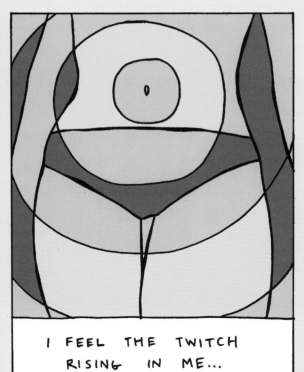

I FEEL THE TWITCH RISING IN ME...

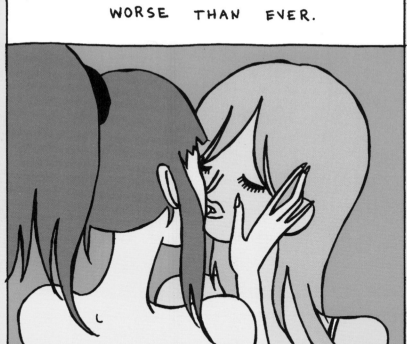

WORSE THAN EVER.

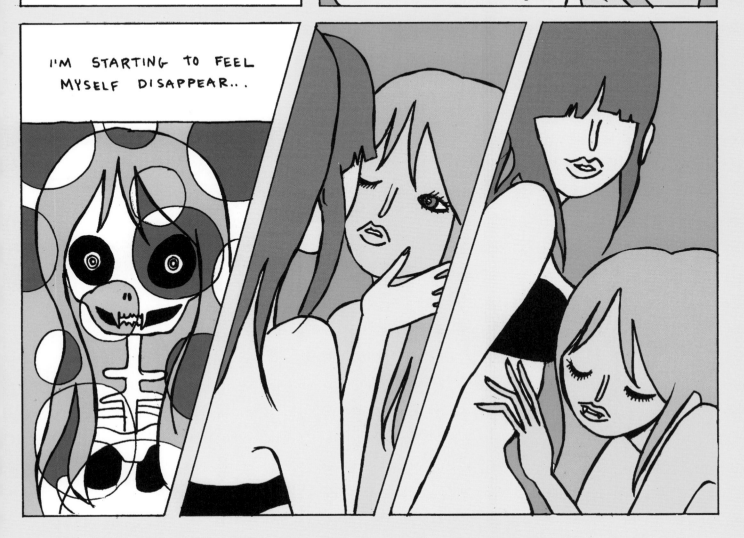

I'M STARTING TO FEEL MYSELF DISAPPEAR...

BUT I'M OFF... SCATTERED...
AND SLOPPY...
I MISS.

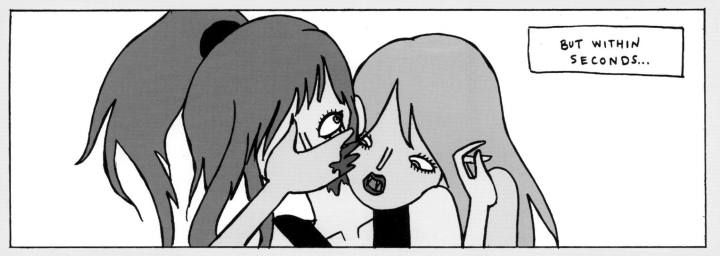

BUT WITHIN SECONDS...

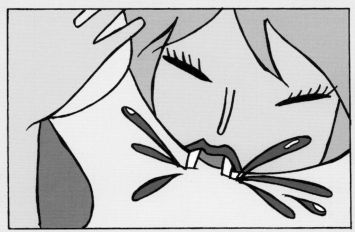

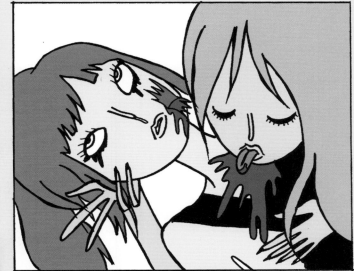

IT'S ALL RIGHT.

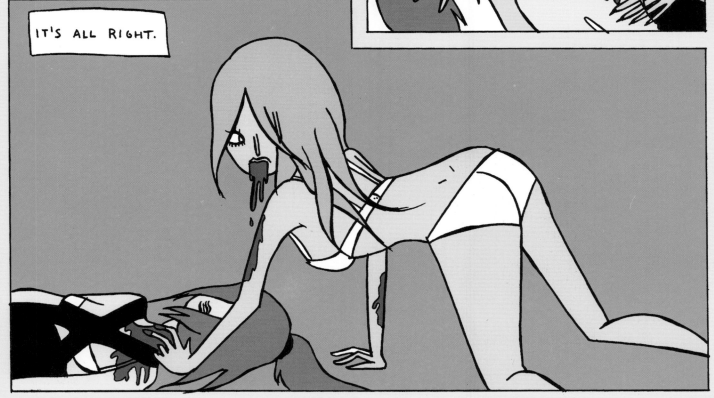

WHAT THE FUCK?

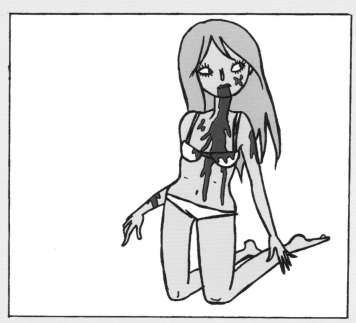

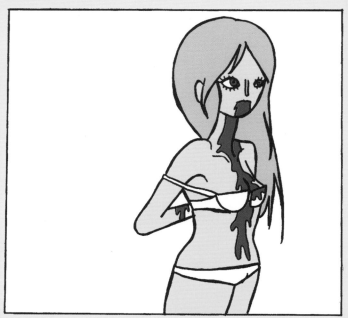

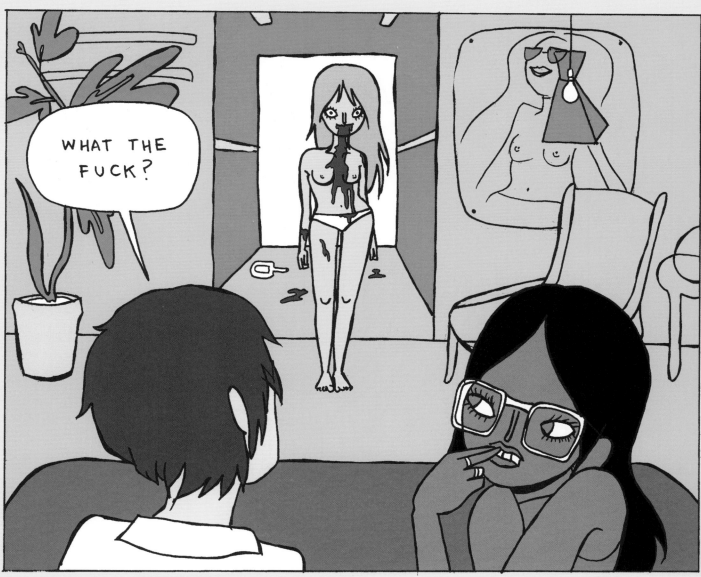

CHAPTER SIX

HISSSSSSSSs...
SSS
!

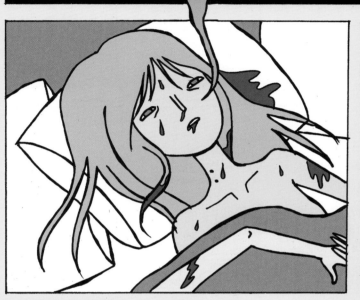

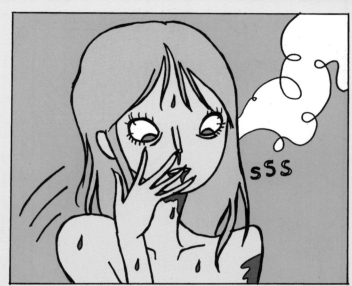

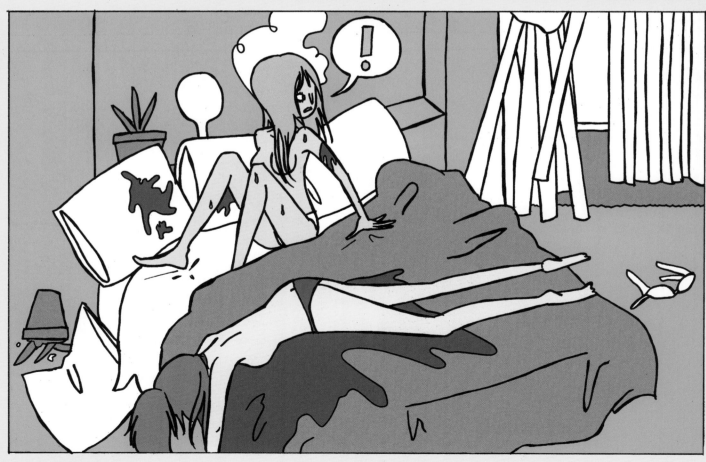

SSS
DING!

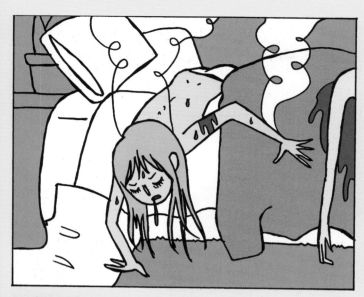

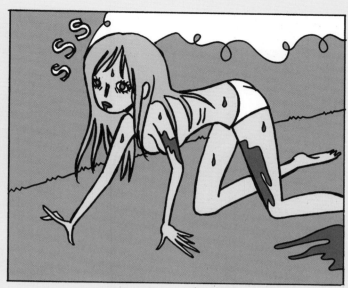

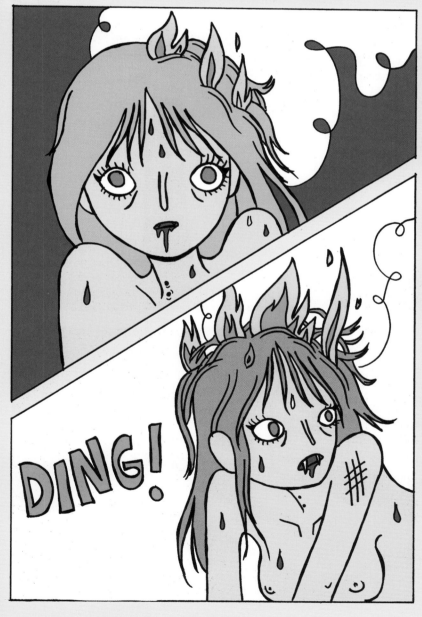

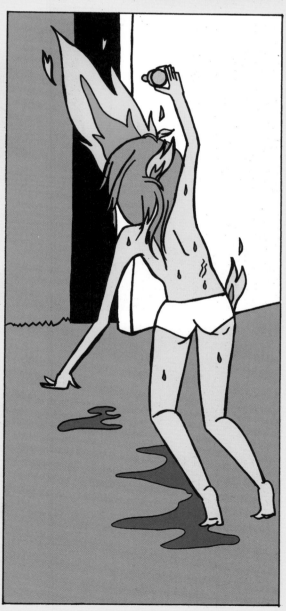

DING!
SSSSSS

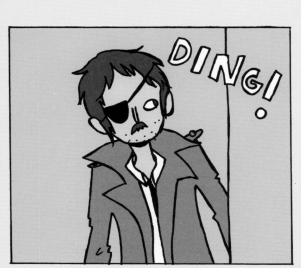

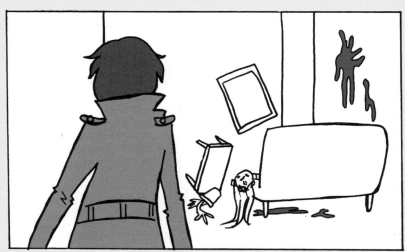

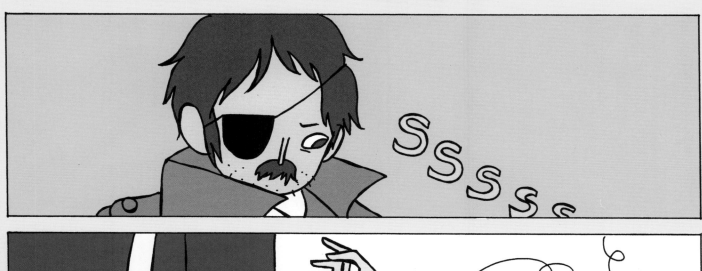

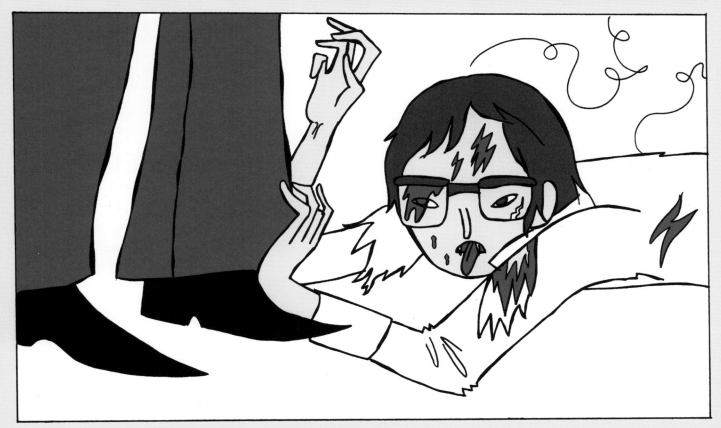

AAAAAA

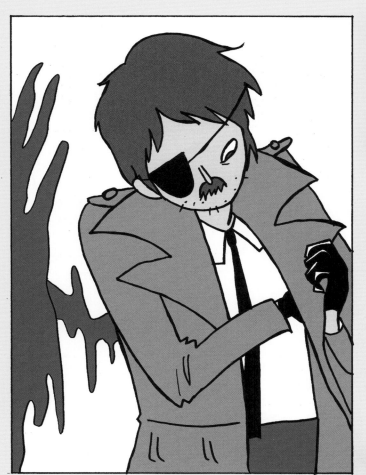

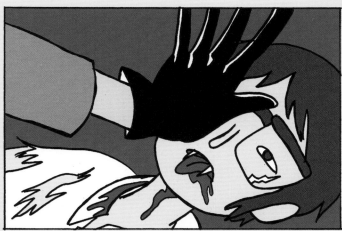

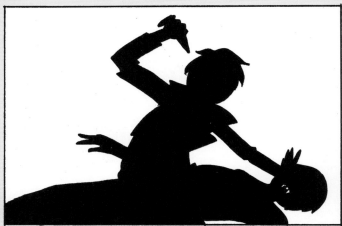

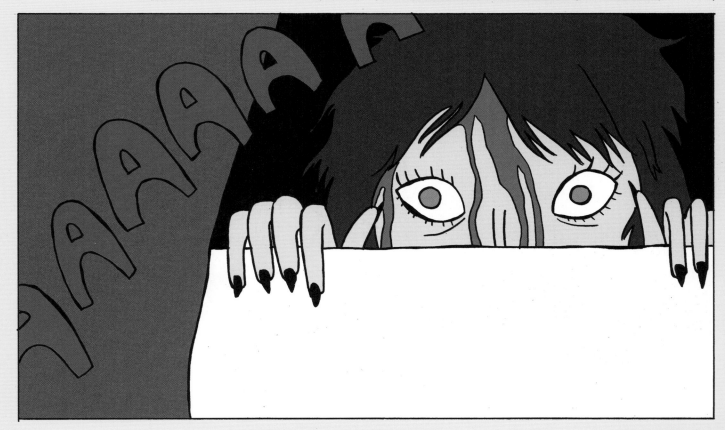

CLOVER?
I KNOW YOU'RE HERE. I WON'T HURT YOU.
YOUR BROTHER SENT ME TO GET YOU HOME SAFE.
I'M SURE YOU DON'T LIKE HURTING ALL THESE NICE PEOPLE...

WHAT DO YOU SAY? HMM?
HISSSSSSS

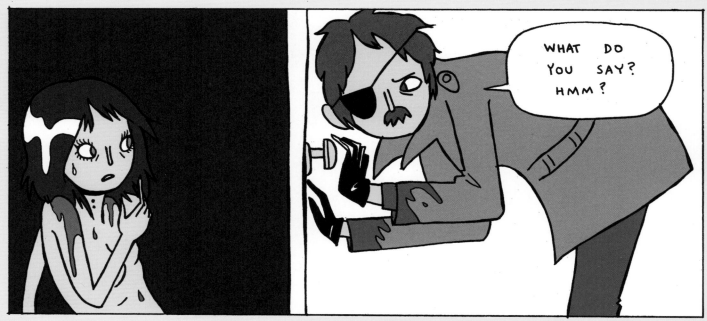

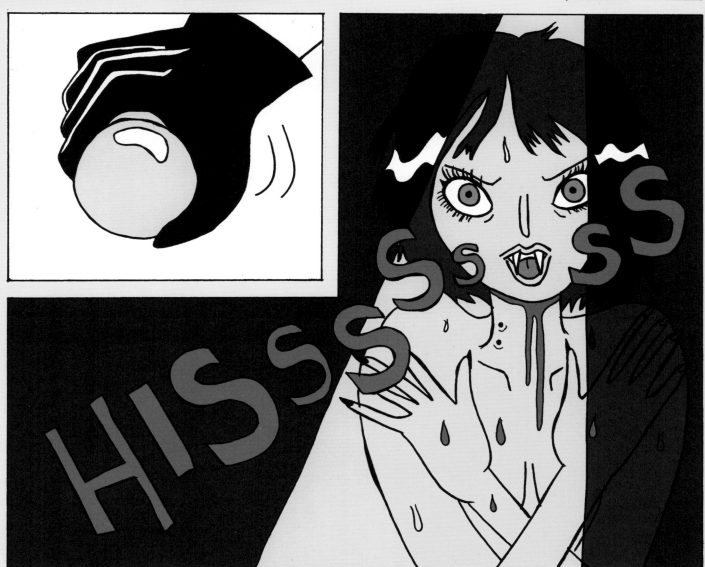

COME ON, NOW!
OW!

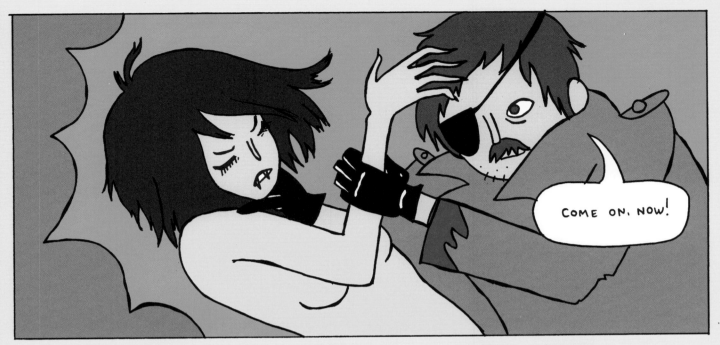

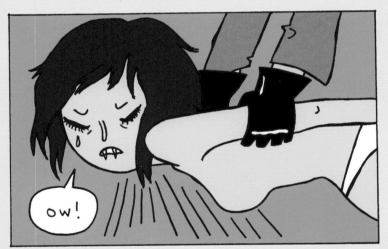

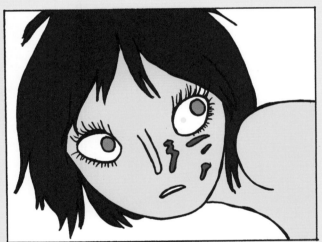

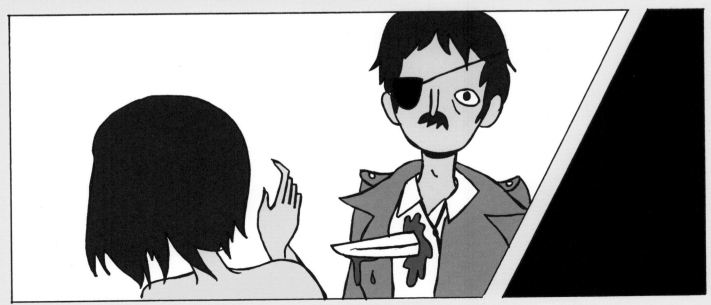

CREAK
WELCOME BACK.

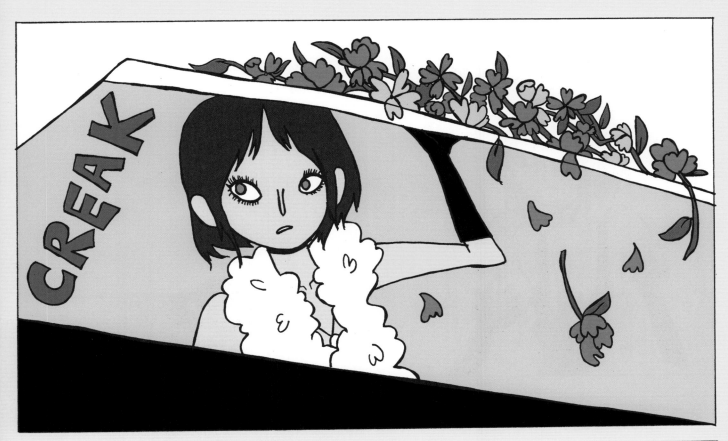

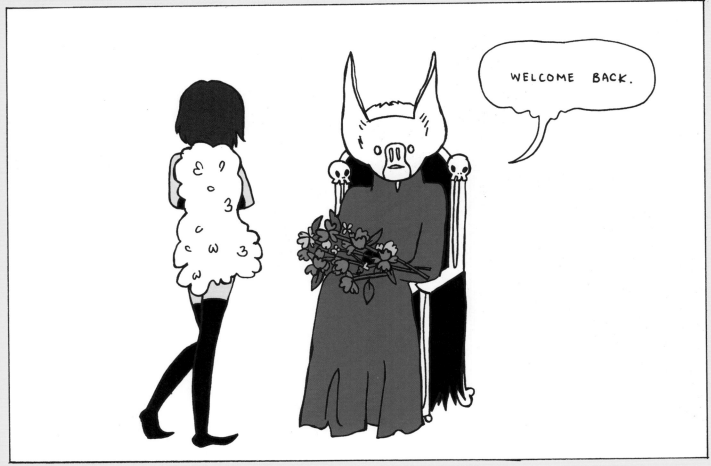

WHAT AM I WEARING...?
I WANT TO MAKE A DEAL WITH YOU.
YOU'RE TOO DANGEROUS FOR THE CITY.
BUT YOUR EVIL IS TOO BEAUTIFUL TO DESTROY...
STAY UNDER COVER AND WE WON'T MEET AGAIN.
BUT WE'LL ALWAYS KNOW WHERE YOU ARE.

WHAT DO YOU SAY?

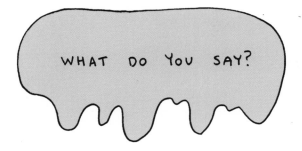

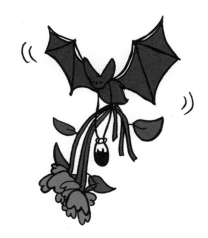

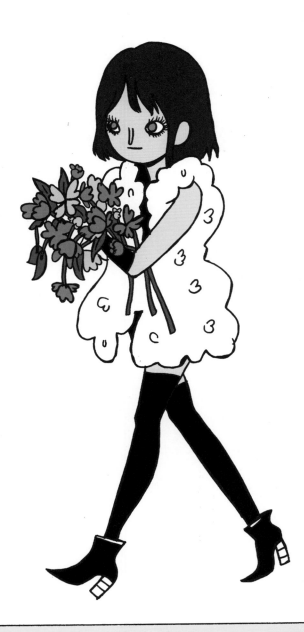

IF IT'S FOREVER,
I DON'T MIND.

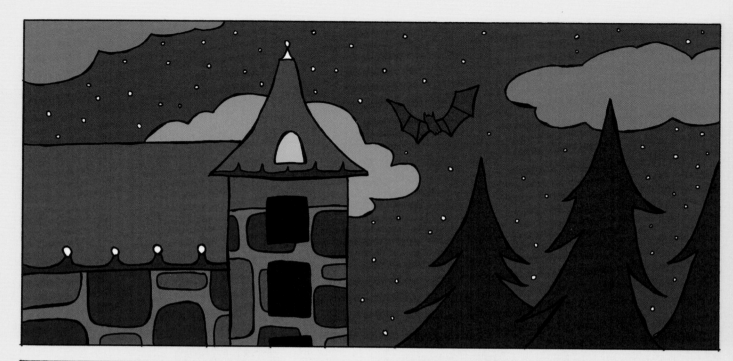

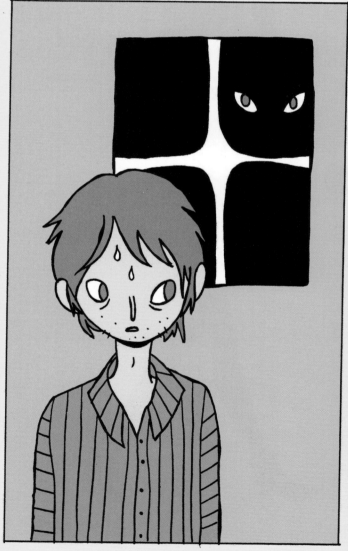

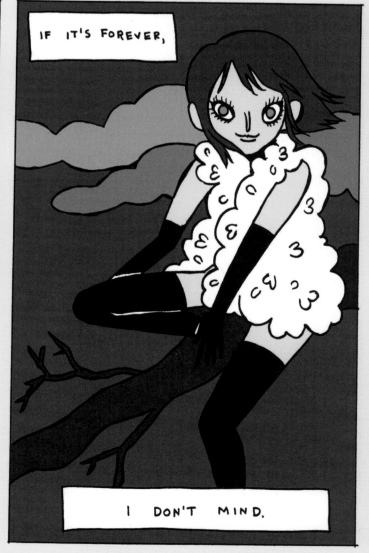

AN ETERNITY WOULDN'T BE LONG ENOUGH TO TORMENT YOU.
FIN

Katie Skelly is a New York City-based cartoonist whose comics include *Nurse Nurse* (Sparkplug Books, 2012), *Operation Margarine* (AdHouse Books, 2014), and the *Agent* webcomic series. She has written and lectured about comics for outlets such as *The Comics Journal*, Fantagraphics Books, Japan Society, The Center for Cartoon Studies, Fordham University, and The New School, and co-hosts the podcast *Trash Twins* with fellow cartoonist Sarah Horrocks. Skelly holds a B.A. in Art History from Syracuse University, and was awarded the Emerging Artist Prize at Cartoon Crossroads Columbus in 2015.

Special thanks: Leeny, Chels, Shannon, Asif, Sarah, Tom, Sally, Jeff & Vijaya, Joggy, Momo, and Anne Louise.